Martha O. Adams

WHAT YOUR HEART NEEDS to KNOW

House of Myrrth 2008
Hendersonville, NC

©2008 by Martha O. Adams
All rights reserved. Published 2008
For copyright permissions, contact: House of Myrrth
Myrrth@bellsouth.net

Printed in the United States of America
ISBN: 978-0-9801418-0-1
Library of Congress Control Number: 2007941454

About the Artist

Julia Denison is currently a senior at Hume Fogg Academic High School in Nashville, TN. She has won national Scholastic awards for her paintings and drawings. In September 2007, her work was selected for an exhibit at the Department of Education, Washington, DC. This is her first cover illustration. She is the granddaughter of Martha Olds Adams.

Blessed be you, universal matter,
immeasurable time, boundless ether, triple
abyss of stars and atoms and generations:
you who by overflowing and dissolving our
narrow standards or measurements reveal
to us the dimensions of God.
–Pierre Teilhard de Chardin–

CONTENTS

CONTENTS

THREE AN INCREDIBLE ART FORM

PRELUDE

It is Enough

Not for me, slim volumes
slipped like grapes
from splitting skins every September.
Volumes, when opened to breathe,
a cork pops in the brain
taste swirls round
the teeth and tongue;
poems nutty with flavor
that hum the mouth
linger on the palate a day, a year
reside within the heart for life...

nor recitations in a trembling voice —
for other hungering bards or jealous
thirsty students, pencils leaden with conceit
or polite and puzzled ladies of the PEO
— pausing, like Adrienne*
to remember where those star shaped
candle holders were bought in 1942;
nor reading me aloud, alone
to claim the measure of
being silent in my skin, burning
in my eyes, tasting the bitter
sweet flavor of words exploring
new geographies joined; or searching with me
to find the phrase that snatches the
breath like foreplays of ecstasy.
No one murmuring my lines
`til senses are engorged

and one is forced to put it down
returning lover bound
to read it through; turning again
to that one page — those awful lines
hooking something deep like fish
asleep invisible beneath the ice —
and then again with reverence, page one,
page two, savoring slowly now and long.

No, mine is the low voltage of steady heat
few lightening bolts. Esoteric rustlings
that lure the mind beyond familiarity;
summer storms simmering on the horizon.
I am too happy, spoiled by his steadfast love
too comfortable to be impoverished by loneliness
that wants company in every potent
detail of the day; too terrified
by women bombed while marketing,
or battered, enslaved for pleasuring;
by children schooled on empty bellies,
by men cardboard boxed beneath trembling
underpasses roaring with our wealth;
too protected from the thousands shuffling
the corridors of greed searching
for a three drag butt, an eye that will connect,
a hand to feed the next quick fix
of food or boozed oblivion.

This is my plenitude...
　　...the fat gray squirrel curled
on the post, a spot of sun
tracing her tail in whiter gray.
I touch the fringe that plays above my brow.
She chews a nut, dropping crumbs

like I drop words, her fingers,
deft like mine, at work
on nubby cylinders of late July corn.
Like big ideas budding,
she disappears in a blink.

...the fat and fading candle
on that dish Mother painted
taking lessons from her neighbor, Maude,
on the ranch in 1922; gilt edged
and blue like the Kansas sky
she knew and loved — a love
intensified under steely Cleveland skies
grayed by refineries that, one day
ignited by the slightest breeze
torched the Cuyahoga. We slept
that night on sooted sheets —
and flowers dainty, pink
her cheeks grew them 'til she
became a stranger in her skin
and all her flowers faded,
withered like her memory; a loss
that stings the heart like it was yesterday.

... or watching Frannie's fingers, rings
enfleshed, flying at the chopping board
stirring bacon, onions, carrots in the holly-
berry red porcelain pot, the sauerkraut
afloat, soaking in the kitchen sink.
I'm setting table, slicing bread
reading recipes or poetry to her
or snatches from a book on acupressure
from the nook above the candle shop in Camden
and always, talk of books; the best

of what we've read.
We mourn the loss of friends
and speak of what it takes to be one
the cost of revelation, the time
the pain when love is lost.

I'm interested in pain
and how to make it go away.
Peering through her nose perched grannies
at the recipe and measuring gin
she says past fifty it's a fact of life
to be ignored, befriended.
Pain… she's cradled it to sleep for years.
She opens the oven door and tucks it all
to bake: the sauerkraut, the fond
exchange of disciplined minds
the gratitude for openings to mysteries profound
and fragrant memories; the hard seeds sown
become the struggled day and bound,
the blessed; all circumstances ripe
as grapes and round as a summer's day
with possibility for distilling on the page.
Sisters in the kitchen, heads of State
inventing ourselves, our governings
and policies — the measure of our care
about each other and the earth.
It is enough.

*refers to Adrienne Rich's poem
"An Atlas of the Difficult World"*

ONE
POWERING

To Longfellow

You stitched the first bright
button of poetry on my shirt
when I was still in braids
when Mother became wrinkled,
her voice broken like the straws
of an old broom; became Nokomis
unwinding her bright threads of rhythm
letting them fly over the waters
of Gitche Gumee lapping nearby.

You embroidered my dresses
with rick rack rhyme predictable
as the colors in the rainbow
you set over the entrance
to my heart; that secret door
that lies beneath the reach
of conscious mind. You gave
the key to Hiawatha. He ran
to fit it in the lock, turned the bolt
and waved me in. The warmth I felt,
still feel now and then, emanates…
ancient coals still whispering
hot words, still drawing me, inviting
me to fan the flame once more.

I wonder if we'd know your name
if you had waited to arrive
until the day when rhyme became
the troubled teen-age foster child
no one wants to claim.

The Church of Poetry

Mr. Garrison, preacherman of Woe-be-gone
clowns behind the mirror, stirs memories
of softer days, of kinder times
sings hymns, blows poems in our ears
calls comedy a lynch mob, a predatory sport
says poetry is church.

I say poetry is up against your mama's skin
when she full of love an' oozin' croon
and when she beat you with a broom!
Poetry is folded in the curve
of daddy's smile, knowin'
his sandpaper chin can rub you raw,
but riskin' it to get the feel
the sound of him;
that rumble in your ear
that whumpin' in his chest
flirting with your hair.
If poetry is church,
that's not how I remember it.

Let me tell you in the church of poetry
no need for fancy clothes
don't have to put your money in.
All you have to do is break your heart, again.
Crack it open wide. Sit there quiet
hold it open for a time
trembling like a winter skin.

When we, who in attacks of vanity
or Spirit blinded, write poetry to sing
in church, here's sometimes how it goes:
you wade in deep, hair rising over your head
you let the moon gospel your soul
you let the waves blues your bones
jazz your blood, adagio your brain
you open up a vein or two
and lie back in that briny No Name ocean
while all your juices mingle, exchange.
Just float there…

…float there,
all your brilliant yammer leaching
and hope the tide will ship out
maybe half your freight,
will bring you in.
Float there, like a three day mama
listening for baby in the other room
'til you begin to hear the mew, the wail, the squall
and then, and then, bewildered, dripping,

No Name glistening on your skin
you grope for paper, pen, and face the glare
that dare-you stare knowing for sure
the blank white page will double-cross you
every time. Knowing all you have to do
is break your knuckles over every line
tease it, toss it, sigh and whine
while words pile up like immigrants
in a tenement, sleeping twenty
in a room for one.

You chicken scratch,
you wart-hog root for grubs.
Ah, chuck it all! Give it up and go to bed.
Forget you may be wakened
in the blackest hour of night
and take it as a sign
that if you haul yourself into the cold
with dream-wet eyes
still floating in the brine
you may hear something
that will set its traces on the page
where you will find them in the dawn
sparkling with a chrism'd shine.

chrism; consecrated oil used for sacraments

Thoughts Un-thought

While weeding in the garden
my thoughts detached; became the keen point
                    digging
in places trod and hardened
became John's dark night burden.
Oh, happy, happy loosening, this digging.

Their roots drove deep and branching
clung to stony soil and sustenance they craved.
Oh, happy loos'ning dancing
my patient tools enhancing
and thoughts un-thought, strengthening as torments
                    braved,
drifted into unseen view
sifted through the openings my keen tool made
and ushered seeds deep into
apertures long overdue.
In softened soil welcoming, they bloom and braid.

On Truth of Skies and Trees

She uses a nutcracker for a pen
pries open the shell of my blind soul
until words, roasted to perfection
fall, salty and gleaming
on the palm of my page-
turning hand. She teases
out tidbits of sagacity
with the pick of her life and wit
until she hears a quiet gasp.

We greedy ones on the long hike
with such wise guides as she
munch on truth of skies and trees
eat water, flower and summer's breeze
stuff our pockets ravenously
for later when the sky has drawn its veil.
Nourished, we find our way
along the winding trail.

Willows

Come…
twine in my lower branches, love
fly the night with me
swaying to heartbeat
rhythms fluttering
up and down trunks
rooted in the sacred soil
of long ago promises.

Like weathered willows
still sprouting green, we tremble
in honeysuckle breezes
of breath, skin, tongue, eyes;
rise with the barn owl's distant call
into the wide sky of body.

Keshia Thomas

The heroism of Keisha Thomas
protecting her taunting enemy spewing hatred ,
was portrayed in the Aug. '96 issue of Life magazine.

Headlong, you race off the pages
of Life, Keshia Thomas, into
the dark heart of poem where
your blackness writes its legacy
clearly as KKK tattoos his arm;
clearly as that tattered
flag of supremacy he drapes
around a heart throbbing fear
across the land. We thought
we'd boxed his kind in pine
but like the slow ooze of pitch
from ancient knots, stubborn
seedlings rise green; another

century's mean sleep is hatching
a parade of blue eyed baby
sixes and sevens with toy guns
proud shouting their "seig heil" salute
blonde curls bobbing
for Daddy's tattooed blessing
his fierce love of "purity." Look
how bleached Mama, sequined angel
of the absolute, smiles.

A hornet's nest, the angry mob,
your white-skinned friends
carry signs condemning hate
demonstrate oblivious to
the conqueror's vein they quarry
in their cause. You lunge
in whirling chaos; sprawl
full flung upon the quivering
manhood of your enemy
your outstretched arms, a mother
eagle's wings around her young
are reminiscent of that other one
who paid the price of bravery humming
blessed are the peace makers.
Blessed are we you walk among us fledglings
on the path of love to show us how.

Who prepared you for this arsony
that inflames the public pages
of a waning century, torching
sacred stereotypes? Sojourner's
outrageous Spirit-sister, Black
Moses of this troubled day
would you reveal the coiled
questions of your heart?
What toll must we pay
to walk with you?

Who Was the Wicked Queen?

Did you ever wonder who she was
the wicked queen with ice chip eyes
who fed Snow White the poisoned apple?
Where did she come from?
When did she become the rigid tree
unbending in the wind? I think
it must have been when all her questions
turned to one before the mirror on the wall
she was undone, her sad heart crumbling
the taste of ashes on her tongue.

Perhaps she thought she was
an uninvited guest to Eve and Lilith's
tea party with platters of juicy
watermelon slices piled high
where laughter-apple dumplings
whispering of nutmeg, clove and coriander
are always being heated up and served
with cream. I know the wicked queen
loves apple dumplings and cream.

Perhaps she was afraid to go
afraid of all those bright seeds
Eve spits shining into the stale air
afraid to watch them scatter
falling in between the cracks

of Adams' ever-changing policies
mythologies, where, taking root
they shatter surfaces, arise
trembling in the light.
Her shining seeds rise, budding inquiry
Why? Why? Why not? Where?
What is it? Who is it for? How does it taste?
When can I have some to share?
Blossoming, they rise sending out
their freedom song like pollen on the breeze
irritating some, providing nectar
for the hidden life of bees.

So when you wonder who she was
ask with me, When do I become
the wicked queen with ice chip eyes
fearful of another's blossoming,
or on the sly slow feed my young
the poisoned fruit?

Surely it is when we teach them how
to stand before that mirror on the wall
asking, Who is the fairest one of all?
we are undone, our sad hearts crumbling
the taste of ashes on our tongues.

Old Speech

Rattling bones on drumheads
griots in West Africa
at their mothers' knee
learn to hear a call that beckons
from a prior harmony
learn to listen to the music
rumbling deep beneath their skin
rhythms of the ancient legends
genealogies and histories
simmering sweet within.

In Mali, on a sheepskin
shaded under thatch and mud
the famous Djeli Baba Sissoko
caresses his guitar.
She is like a book I strum
the repertoire of all the griots gone before.
The kora, the drum, my balafone
all speak the ancient tongue.

Making hollows in the sand
legs, slim tents of polished ebony
the people lean to hear
wise Djeli Baba speak. They hum
him back. Men fondle burnished rungus
hewn from thorned acacia tree
knobbed to challenge all ferocity,
woman sass or infidelity.

Proud cinnamon skin Mama
squatting at the charcoaled pot
stirs the honeyed milk for chai
rakes the glowing embers
keeps the waning flame alive.

He speaks aside to me;
Coached by our elders in the praise songs
stories of nobility, how to arbitrate
the squabbles that arise in families
explain the unexplainable
black cats covering the moon
our bodies are the looms
that spin the stories; voices
shuttling sing song secrets
of the old mythologies. Between
the cool white warp of morning
and the red threads of the fire
we weave wisdom
we weave the lineage of the clan
and noble families. In garments
fringed with laughter we teach
our people how to live,
live productively, cohesively.

Mama, squatting at the pot
rakes the glowing embers.

Encircled by his children, twenty five
four wives, all circumcised
declitorized, to end the roaming eye
the budding blossom of desire,
he sings his ancient stories.
Heads brightly turbaned,
faces glisten in the heat.
They know that listening
is like the making of batik
that flows in rivers `round their limbs;
is strong enough to cradle babies in
endures the pounding of the millet
the tumbling stream, the scorching sun;
speaks in white and silent spaces
like the margins of a book.
They keep his words
from falling off the page.

Some only understand the music
not the words. For them I paint
the story on her strings. He strums...
She sings them to the present
to the campfire of the ancients.
And painting gestures in the air
his canvas holds no hint of the despair
that molders in his bones,

for in a nearby village on a Sunday
late, they gather not to celebrate the griot
but to crank the generator.
They need no bones for drumming.
Locust-like it thrums into the skies
children racing beetles cease their play.
Now the moon is clouded
acrid fumes arise. The circled feast
of flaming faces drenched with griot lore
is gone. Here the balafone is silent
kora speaks no more. They stare
as crackling voices spring to life.
White magic shadows dance
against the wooly sweatered night.
Ghostly people captured weekly
weave them wanting what is new
as they view another episode of *Dynasty*,
study legends of the white man
dubbed in French

while young cinnamon skin Mama
hums the chai, stirring wisdom
raking it alive. *Listen to me, son*
she speaks low into his ear.
Among all things in all the world
only one, hear me now, only one
gives birth to its Mama.
Trying hard to understand
he traces patterns in the sand
distracted by the lure
of the legends of the white man
flickering in the distant dark.
What do it mean, Mama?

His chin between her fingers and her thumb
she locks into his eyes with hers
he plumbs the depths of her
What do it mean?

Speech… speech births its Mama
straps her to its back, she says.
Think on it and we will talk again.
Think on it, my son.
And as she pours two cups of chai
he rattles bones; somber rhythms
dry against the drum.

What is Holy?

*written January 14, 1991 as the United Nations
resolution supported by Congress, gives
President George H.W.Bush authority
to go to war with Iraq.*

Ice encrusted rage
sends weeping warriors
to "holy death"
splintered souls anonymous;
fear trigger-fingering
the spooked sand
in wind-whipped clouds
across the moonless midnight sky.

As I'm wondering what is holy,
ancient constellations
brilliant all these million years
guide the desert rat
the salamander, snake;
still inform the desert rose
exploding into life
as this new strata of bones
fuels future wars.

I Wear the Women of Bosnia Like a Blister on my Heart

When he was two and barefoot
drunk on dandelions
bottom heavy and
cooing at the sky
my youngest dearest-last
tipping about the new mown grass
uttered a scream
that echoes down
twenty six years
of days and dreams.

I still replay the frenzied scene:
my frantic efforts to console
not knowing what had ripped his soul
until my searching fingertips
read the agony imprinted
on his every step;
a moon of skin
rising like a yeasty bun.
He could not say
what had been done.
The mower, stilled
sat steaming in the sun.
Guilt adorns the memory
like fresh flowers on a grave.

Anne Taylor Fleming, all genteel
mowed our blinders down
on last night's news.
We stepped, barefoot
on the white-hot steel
of her scalding words
and Bianca's fearless lens.
They had to know
what had ripped his soldier's soul
and etched the raging question
into our fattening holocaust history.

Why the women?
Why rape the women
the little girls? Why?
The planet reels
at his empty faced reply
If I had not
I would be shot.
Freedom, stilled
sits steaming in the sun.

I wear the women of Bosnia
like a blister on my heart
fresh flowers on my grave.

The Voice of Rachel
SWS-87

*A voice is heard in Ramah lamenting and weeping
bitterly; it is Rachel weeping for her children, refusing to
be comforted, because they are no more. Jeremiah 31:15;
Matthew 2:18*

*Quotes and story from an interview with SWS-87 on
National Public Radio; 1996.*

I am SWS-87, eleven birthday candles blown
in a place I didn't know was heaven
a place I just called home. Ledici,
Ledici, Bosnia it sang my tongue!
Four birthdays, no candles
in a place I now call hell.

It was April 1992 they came,
spring rain like wool on the mountain.
They took me to a filthy cell
for "interrogation purposes."

Accused of lying,
my girl body quivered like a sapling tree.
They stripped me bare
climbed me there
five rough men, a pimpled boy
always one laughing
watching, pressing his gun
to my head. My god, the smell
of them, their swollen members
blades between my legs.
They numbered me SWS-87.
I survived to tell.

They took me to my school
where I had learned my numbers
how to read and write and play
and say my name, and locked me
with the others; girls, cousins
lamenting mothers, Auntie B.
We were ashamed. At first
we hardly spoke, the bitter weeping
of our dreams provoked the drunken
guard. We soon became their raping pool
they used us every day. For me
it happened in the night. They took
me to the gymnasium, and hell
went on, and on, and on
eight months or more.

But I had learned my numbers
how to read and write and play
and say my name. I am SWS-87
and I survived to tell.

One night they set me naked
on a table like a jug of wine
commanded me to dance
for Montenegran officers.
One purchased me for
two week's pay and took me
to his private hole to have his way.

When terror finally bled
into the chambers of the law
our woman stories were "too
embarrassing to consider in court".
For **our woman shame, our guilt**
many, even sisters want to silence us.
"There are things outsiders
should never know," they say.
I tremble speaking out. My daily fear,
reprisals on my friends and family
the ones who have not disappeared.
But I am now fifteen. I have
learned my numbers
how to read and write and play
and say my name. I am SWS-87
I am not ashamed.

Karen Armstrong

After reading Armstrong's A History of God

Aptly named for hauling rare
books home from libraries
around the globe to send
their weight page by page
through the genius of her mind
(they become the captain
she, a tugboat churning steadily
through historic tides)

she pulls along behind
a string of barges
broad, clumsy, worrying
about control at every narrowing
where currents race
or placid widening where
rocky bottomed shallows
gossip, stuttering in
the stale winds of certainty
each barge identified
by the freight it bears;
its unique view of truth.

Quite an endless line
stretching out behind this
well captained tug.
Her steadfast sagacity
the sobriety of her scholarship

requires intense listening to
every point of view.
She counts her charges off
so none are left behind
as mothers, teachers do:
Pagan, Catholic, Protestant
Muslim, Jew, Orthodox, Reformed,
Unitarian, Philosopher, Scientist,
agnostic and mystic, too.
She guides us down that
long dynamic pining through
the wide and awkward
turning of millennia
past a landscape bleak
and Spirit desolate
that sets us pondering
the somber view:

black sails of tribal idolatries
flapping in the anguished wind;
catastrophes nourished by
our neon need for more,
for more, for more;
God's final obsequies,
the closing of that ruined door;
and there, on the inflowing tide
she tugs us up the River Compassion,
leaves us at the dock of no return.

No Choice but to Choose

Nameless One
your names echoing
echoing down long stained corridors
walled by love and hate
faith and fear
pulsate in hidden springs
ever freshening
ascend like bubbles from the pot
in clouds of steam
like feathers sprung from
milkweed pods, from cottonwood
floating on the wind.

I call you by the dearest name
I know, with confidence
and find you here, singing glory
a chorus silent as snowflakes
falling from the moon rising

like a biscuit over the mountain crest
or shining through the ocean's
cellar door at dawn, luminous.

Earthquake, soft as my gaze
sifting through the screen,
you are Eternal Wonder
charging the universe
with energies endless as waters
roaring over the curving cataract.

You pour your nothingness
in thundering whispers into
the dim and desolate recesses
of the heart, finding only drops
of nectar there. You give us
everything... and nothing but
no choice but to choose.

Slippery Eel

leaping for life
just as I think I've landed you
you wiggle away
beyond my grasp
my hands
my heart
slick with memory
wanting
the electric jolt of you
that shocks me
out of my skin.
You keep me fishing
for the love of It.

Chastened

A friend loaned me a book
she knew I'd like
about the settling of Florida.
"I'd give it to you
but it's very hard to find.
It's one of those you want to keep."
It became high adventure
read out loud before we went to bed
yet soothing too, like Good Night, Moon
or Uncle Wiggly; Huckleberry Finn.
By the end we wanted one
to pass along and one to keep for lending.

One cloudy day we pulled into
the permanent flea market
for curiosity, and just to pass the time.
I saw the "Used Books" sign,
smelled that respectable and learned mold

the mites with Ph D's
the yawns, the sighs and sneezes,
dreams and crumbs and coffee spots
all brittle-yellowing.

This rabble mob nearly undid me.
I heaved a sigh, said
to a last week's dumpling of a woman
standing by, her muddled apron
resigned as the expression she wore,
"Do you work here?" She bore
her snaggle-tooth, her unwashed hair
somewhat unfamiliar with a comb
with an air of dignity. "Can you
tell me how the books are organized?"
implying the impossibility.

She said, "What are you looking for?"
A Land Remembered, by Patrick Murphy
I replied. "You must mean Patrick Smith"
she said, reaching for two books
on a shelf nearby; one cloth, one paper back.
Dumbfounded, chastened, I remain
and she continues teaching me to refrain
from judging any book by its covering.

My Friend,

grief is a hungry one ton bear
riding on your back
growling in your ear,
"Turn your head!
Look me in the eye
or I'll tear you limb from limb!
Are you listenin'? Look at me
or I'll sleep your days
I'll woo your wife
I'll grizzle your chin
I'll hibernate your life.
Are you listenin'?"

He sighs, remembering
his other life. "I'd rather
climb on down, go find my friends
pick us some berries plump and blue
than spend my days alone
claws anchored in your skin
and eating you."

Young Cellist

My morning coffee steams
images of that young cellist
we saw last night in the high
school auditorium. Surely she dreams
this morning, too, remembering
the thumping of her heart
the fleeting fear it might show
beneath the glow of her black sequined
gown, the wide skirt ballooned
with petticoats, flowing
around her as she strode onstage
carrying her cello like a shield.
She took her nervous bow
behind six pink hydrangeas
blossoming in a row.

This greening virtuoso
with grace still timid, undefined
settled on the chair

briefly tuned to the oboe's A
raised her bow and nodded
for maestro to begin
as she withdrew into Lalo's skin
exploring yet again, paths
meandering within the Prelude
of his labyrinthine concerto.
Her heart became another member
of the orchestra. Her fingers flew!
And with a final flourish of the bow
a smile grew between the two
hydrangeas blooming in her cheeks.

The coffee steams… I see
myself fifty years ago, clutching
my cello with shaking knees
throat tightening before
the hometown audience. Last night
this vibrant memory intertwined,
became a silent river inviting me
to breathe with her into the notes
into the solid conjugation of string
and fingerboard and bow;
to enter on the moon-rise
of her lush vibrato, a holy place
I'd left behind not long ago.

Anna Wittstruck has continued her studies
at Princeton University

TWO
THE IMMORTAL WHEEL

What Your Heart Needs to Know

One night, drowning in a dream
words appeared like a lifeguard's line
thrown out to me. I reached for them
breathed them in, afraid
they'd drift away.
Listen! they said…
Listen! The earth will tell you
in the middle of the night
what your heart needs to know.

Go to the quiet room inside
where you become
mockingbird drowsing
in moon shadow dappled
over her young — become
the engineer, his dreams and yours
lifting the long, low whistle
of the nightly train — the breeze
sifting through long needled pine
stirring fireflies' urgent signaling.

There, rise from dew rich grass
become the grass's stubborn
need to grow — the dew's
inevitable drawing down
and nurturing, only to be drawn
up and out to disappear again

and yet again to gather in and fall
one with all things moist
tied to the moon and flowing.

You, dancing the ribbon of rivers, tides.
You, becoming fish, snake, spider.
Within her night's work glistening
become her patient hunger.
Wait...watch. Silent, feel the quake
the tremulous shudder;
become moth's last quivering.

First breaths, last breaths
everywhere, you become
there in the quiet room inside
one with all life's measured regularities
the slow extravagance of breath within,
beside you, carved in memory
or even possibility. There
words and signs curl in
like butter under a hot knife
to melt and fuel the fevered
greening edges of your life.

Come... the earth will tell you
in the middle of the night
what your heart needs to know.
Go to the quiet room inside
and you are home.

What Lies Above, Lies Below

As the purple eye of iris opens
blinking beneath an obsidian sky
the shy bronze fox emerges
from her dusky den, her pups
spilling and tumbling on spring's
trampoline of green. She watches
over them like the holy ghost
with agate eye. A cardinal sings.
Nesting blue birds fling
lapis lazuli streaks mid-air.
An opal-throated hummingbird
the color of tourmaline darts
among a galaxy of lilies
orange-flecked and buttery
cascading down the hill. Coal-
glistening, a cricket shrills repeatedly.

At night when all this quickening
of life is stilled, dewdrops
about to spill from needled pine
gleam quietly beneath the moon
a web of pearls spun
for just this twilight's reckoning
and down among the hushed
and rainbow'd coral reefs
jeweled necklaces of fish
are strung and re-strung endlessly
within the shimmering turquoise sea
and just as quietly below

deep within their molten rookery
grow amethyst, jasper, obsidian
danburite, emerald, ruby and coal
agate, bloodstone, topaz, opal
moonstone, lapis and carnelian.

What lies above, lies below
what lies without, within.

I close my eyes and there
as if illuminated on a screen
flowers bloom, cardinals sing.
Do you find it so?
All the gardens I have ever seen
I wear behind my eyes
gardens tilled and sprung
from where quick-silver runs
within the humus of each gardener's
heart. There, in mine I find
each sunset, sunrise blossoming
like peonies flung across the skies.

And you, I know, have sat like me
around the campfire of the interior
where friends, some here, some gone
gather to retell stories kindled
like firewood cut and stacked
against a winter spell of loneliness.
Warmed there, I see love
leaping through the flame
hear hearts echoing across
the void of unsaid things
and in the silence of all this mystery
the soft enunciation of my name
coming from the purple eye of iris opening.

What lies above, lies below
what lies without, within.

Hitch-hike the Hubble With Me

Oh, you much-knowing tube
more valuable than any scepter
Johannes Kepler

Come, step out and go in
where it's quiet inside
outside on a starry night.
We'll hitch-hike the Hubble
make it our ark to sail in the dark
between stars through a space
small as a dime at seventy feet —
a period, a dot, an oil spot
on that vast black canvas of sky
painted with glory
lightening and thunder
— on and on sail through
an unfolding story to an
uncertain place, we'll wander.

Now, focused and mirrored and magnified
through that wee window
grown large, can you say
what you see in that vast nothingness?

Thousands, ten thousands more stars?
Look again. Can it be? They're not stars at all
but un-numbered galaxies!
Whirling, spinning reflections of light
each with its billions of suns.
Hundreds, thousands never before seen
in that spit of a space between.

Gazing with me at eternity
out of touch with time
out of our minds, let's
linger in wonder a while.
When we debark from our far-seeing ark
that black spit of a speck
of a spot in the sky
will keep sweeping stars
into our souls and we'll never repeat
the common conceit
there's nothing there at all.

Light

Igniting waves of possibility
through dimensions yet unknown
this elfin siren preens
before the baffled mirror of the mind.
She is a tease! Ask Galileo
Newton and Feynman.
Ask the wooly haloed Einstein
Lao Tzu, who called her name "unknown"
"The Tao." Inquire of Plato, even John
who tells us how to walk with holy light.
Ask Najm Razi, though worlds apart
for whom she rises, shining
in the skyscapes of the heart.

She rides currents of the mind
strung out like autumn leaves astride
a rippled stream disturbed by stone
yet is the rippling wave beneath —
an orphan wave whose only home is possibility.
Pure form, she is no thing,
this fairy sprite not made of anything
we can put beneath the lens,
but dancing now and then within
the inner universe of body, heart and mind
we see her sing — her silent melody
illuminating everything.

This Elegant Adagio

Under the Carolina sun
I swim laps snorkled and masked
entranced by the prism'd
warp and weft loomed
on the floor below;
a net of light
an undulating allemande,
amorphous grand right and left
slow coupling and uncoupling.

This elegant adagio
invites a silent opening like one
through which I'd passed before
the day I knew that I could fly
when I was four, arm-warmed beside
grandmother's knee, when suddenly
suddenly! ABC was CAT and DOG!

I swim laps through this same
aperture and know with certainty
that sun and moon and stars, all
minstrels of the harmonies above;
that rocks and soil, plants and trees
and air, all drops of moisture,
every sip I drink dehumidified

through clouds and dinosaurs,
that creatures visible, invisible
everywhere defined by life or breath,
this awesome all, are inextricably entwined.

And we among this cosmic choir
ecumenical? We are but one —
one conjugation of the Word
one spark of that first light enshrined
in touch, in thought, in smile
in doing what we can to reconcile
and mend the tattered web
we've been so quick to rend.
It is a humbling swim.

Through Water I Am

Before light or earth, night or day
before wild bush, or tree or flower
before we awakened from brine and clay
before sun or moon, sky or air
darkness was upon the face of the deep
and the Spirit of God brooded there.
Over the dark vapors
God breathed, and there was water.
The Cherokee say *when the earth began*
there was just water.
All the animals lived above
and in the crowded sky no room
remained to live or nest or play.
Hindus create the world this way;
a vast dark ocean
washed upon the shores of nothingness
and licked the edges of night.
Original Mother; matrix of formation
and devastation...water! as it was in the beginning
is now and ever shall be, powering
the immortal wheel between earth and sky.
Water! Forever unchanged in quantity.

Through this drop of water, I am connected, I am
to that first breath brooding over the deep
to that vast dark ocean licking
the edges of nothingness.
I drink this water and become earth and sky
wind and sea, snow and ice and creeping glacier

become one with dew drop, with flower and bee
with elephant and hummingbird
one with all whose laughter, whose voice
whose music I have ever heard
with all life everywhere that bathes, that drinks
and breathes, expelling vapors into the air.
My breath rises along with theirs, mingling
with cloud, eagle, hawk and wren
gathering density and falling once again.
Water, from ancient aquifer, drawn up through
root and leaf and stem — filtered through
bodies and lungs and skin.

I drink this breath of ancient ones gone extinct
cave man, mastodon and dinosaur. I drink
the steaming jungles of Equador
and all life teeming deep within. I drink
meadows, mountain springs and boggy sedge.
I drink every winged thing that feeds
along the water's jagged edge. I drink
all birthing, breathing things gone before
living now and yet to come.

I swim through water as once
I did in mother's womb connecting her
and me with every mother reaching
back and forth through time.

I swim connected to star-fish,
to great sea turtles, dolphin
whale, shark and manatee
to all the vibrant multitude of living coral reef.
I swim connected to all things finned
or crabbed and crawling
through the braided grasses of the deep.

Bathed in moon and candlelight
I sit to bread and wine, gazpacho soup
and eat this water, rich with wonder and delight.
I eat sun and rain and fertile soil.
I sip the love of a farmer's toil
and if you stop and think of it
through water I am connected, I am
to water that may have touched the lips
of Hildegard, of Julian
of Christ, Gautama Buddha
Muhammed, Krishna or Abraham.
Connected, I am to water carried
through blazing heat and served to them
by women rapt and listening at their feet.
To all of this, through water
I am connected, I am.

Antarctica

Great
  White
    Walrus
stern whiskered in ice
librarian of planetary secrets
we probe your glaciered crevices
biopsy the deadly
midnight blue of your womb
waters, electrified by the wonder
of your progeny — hermaphrodite,
phoenix, sagittary, shimmering*
`neath the ruthless bow of your belly.

We feel life jump within us.
You make mothers of us all.
We breathe a million years
encapsulated in snowflakes;
sighs crystallized before the Christ;
uncork the layered centuries
with trembling hands
like doctors, midwives bring forth life.
We try, unbiased now, to study history
thin sliced beneath a lens.

The news is this… our mother melts
and like most mothers
contains grief deep within
the tissue of her dreams.
Mothers never want to hurt the children
see them suffer even those who've battered her
assuming like the prodigal
she'll always be around.
She knows our underwater ballet
has but a nine month run
when like the penguin we soar
into the light to dance
upright and awkward stealing
pebbles for our thrones forgetting
all the cosmic messages
imprinted in our bones.

*hermaphrodite: anything comprised of a combination of
diverse or contradictory elements; phoenix: anything of
surpassing beauty, excellence; sagittary: arrow shaped

Dawn at Key Largo

The white haired woman
in the periwinkle hooded jacket
yawns to her spot among the coral rocks
turns her cheek into the rain-washed breeze.
In the shallows, the great white heron
stalks. Complaining gulls tack and yaw
settling on blue roofed cabanas.
The osprey pair perch pole-top
on their nest of sticks and plastic bags.
Cumbrous pelicans glide
like a fleet of brown-winged barges
guiding comical wide-footed bodies to land
with ease atop four round pilings
crusted with barnacles and weeds.
Doves coo in distant banana trees
the smell of sea and coffee in the air.
Water continues its antediluvian colloquies
with ancient coral hewn and piled, dead
and sprouting grasses now, along the shore.

The Cuban fishermen arrive
in the black pick-up, sleepy wife and baby
at the wheel. She waits while silently
they transfer rod, reel and boxes
of frozen bait to the battered white boat
with the black canopy. Pulling on tall
rubber boots, they wave and steal

into the widening crack of the sky's horizon,
reddening. The baby cries.
As the fertile yolk of morning
breaks upon the ocean floor
the man in the straw hat with knotted rope
around the crown, who loves to paint
appears on his old black bicycle
to gaze into today's monochromatic
palette with wistful thoughts
of halcyon days and what's to come.

Three sailboats with gently tilting masts
moored peacefully off Rodriguez Island
sleep on.

Hurricane Wanda

That rowdy wench named Wanda
ten times ten more powerful
than Flagler's train on its bronco
busting ride to fame, riches and rust
grizzled up the Keys last fall
the palms and hardwoods
bowed, uprooted, or splintered
by her iron knuckled fist.

Like a giant osprey swooping
down to snatch its prey, she
picked the ficus, sapodilla, bottle brush
and orchid trees clean of every leaf
sucking briny marrow from
their broken-open bones.
The snarling ocean lunging
for her breast, climbed up
the mangroves beating them

like kettle drums — a hundred
symphonies of them
and cymbals, crashing in the wind.

We think we run the show
'til something greater than all of us
combined comes roaring through
leaving its calling card behind.

Now three short months
have offered up their grace.
This morning on my dawn patrol
I found a sapodilla soft and round;
caught a passing fragrance on the breeze…
the orchid tree, magenta heart
beating wildly, lush fuchsia horns
blowing tender melodies.

The Potter

Remembering Wendy

Her face, honest as a pitchfork
announces the need for solitude
for evening walks throwing long thoughts
across the river meandering
through her neighborhood.
Her brown eyes, serious as September
abide beneath a brow carved
like some famous president I can't recall...
Is it Honest Abe? Yes, Abraham
remembered for the hope and dread
of our first freedom ride. Like his
her brow is furrowed with a life
that runs deep as a plow and wide
through the fields of her years.
She wears her graying hair
with a farm-wife's dignity that mystifies
the bleached, streaked and dyed.

I wonder, when she was building
the country road of her thirty five years
straight down the neon noise of New York City
did she even then wear faded jeans
pink cotton shirts with nine white buttons
strutting down the front like a small town band?
I'm thinking P.S. 183 frowned on pearls
crystals and sandals, baby blue
with all that toe on show.
Perhaps her higher school of music

and art encouraged the bending
into the being of herself
which would explain the glasses
secured by moss green fabric akin
to the color of her backpack
where she keeps her love affair
with form, fire, and function simmering
like apples turning to butter in the fall.

Her Quaker hands, wedded to clay
to the worn oak handle of every day
rest now, quiet as kittens in her lap
a sign of the peace she bears
within a life familiar as a barn-yard cat
with uncertainty. She yearns for love
for being loved; conveys an air of honesty
that worries when the gift of it
is not returned in kind.

Is she happy here? She seems unsure.
Was Lincoln happy in Washington?
I see him longing for the day
when he could spend the nub of time
still left to him, on his wind-whipped
Illinois farm close to the clay.
And where would she like to live?
Wherever it is, I haven't been there yet.
I'm going out to Santa Fe where I can be
close to the clay. Close to the clay.

Time Goes By

O Time, your spell is meaningless
when one can feel the intelligence
of every living thing so keen
upon the heart it cuts all ties
to your authority.
Whoever said time goes by
never suckled at a mother's breast
where you gush warm
and dribbling down the chin
collapsing in to baby-dream oblivion
become that placid wide-eyed stare
piercing the heart of truth.

Whoever said time goes by
never was a child
squatting ankle deep
the cold creek's stony clatter
shocking warm and rosy flesh;
two living things encountering

fresh wildernesses of the other sphere.
Here, time is tadpoles
and tiny darting things, liquid laughter
stone on stone, and water bugs
skittering on surfaces invisible.

Full, full, unmeasured and un-measuring
to live this fierce attentiveness
unclaimed by the jealous I
where even time untainted and untamed
must die to fearless wonder.

Whoever said time goes by
never waited, like I, for the days
the weeks to pass 'til he
would come and break me open
with tender kisses and secret whisperings;
or watched from the corner of the eye
time rocketing, slam
against the wall between
him sudden gone
and me alone again, slow learning
the dangerous new math
of one becoming two — both
unconscious of that day when
this equation will reverse itself
and time becomes again un-moveable
the exiled solitude of one, forever cleft.

Whoever said time goes by
never stood before a perfect spider's web;
observed the quiet, poised architect
and saw the world, the universe entire
pearled in dew; or wondered
spirit lifted by the song
of cardinal, wren or mockingbird
at such effusive happiness rendered
flagrant on the solemn air
or touched the backward pinking parabola
of Rubrum lily's spotted arrogance
each stamen shod in wee slippers
cinnamon and dancing with butterfly
blue, blue as the Carolina sky
who probes its fragrance patiently
and pirouettes away

full, full, unmeasured and un-measuring
to live this fierce attentiveness
unclaimed by the jealous I
where even time untainted and untamed
must die to fearless wonder.

Praying Mantis

astride magenta cosmos frond
you ride the breeze, stalking the fattest
black and yellow bumble bees
nab, and calmly dine on them
one bite at a time oblivious
to their silent struggle to survive.
Languidly you probe the golden sacrament
of sun-dusted pollen, powdering petals
aloft thin stemmed acolytes
green and trembling beneath
our blue candled sky.

I find you resting now
hands joined in prayerful repose.
Your head, triangular, turns to consider me.
You indulge my curiosity, my need
to know, to see — allow the gentle stroking
of your green-leaf body hammock slung

between the branching architecture
of your spindly frame. I search in vain
for eyes — fetch Pa's old magnifying glass.

Beneath the parabola
of your twin antennae, magnified
I see two pinpricks of black intelligence
gazing into me. No world, no universe
no night or day exists but this —
this silent communiqué between
two lucid minds awestruck and briefly joined.
Like the bumblebees, I am consumed
become green velvet hung upon the breeze.

Considering the Lily

The Mayans said the sun at night
hides inside the jaguar. I say, in day
you swallow it and let it play
within your curving veil
fletched with gold and dew.
I join hummingbirds who
drink daily from your grail.
Bees prosper at your font
as do butterflies, ants
and creatures infinitesimal.
I look at you and God is visible
in elegant extravagance.

For each stately blossoming
twelve hours of light is all
you've been bestowed
before your beauty fades
and you must die to go within
to grow in dark of pod.

Such undeserved frugality
twelve hours of light
and in that slender stem of time
you, unselfconsciously sublime
are simply opening
conferring hospitality.

Pink Canna Lilies

for Lois

"I have some pink Canna lily bulbs to share…
stop by when you are out"
the pale widow said, still trying
to repair the days he'd dimmed
by leaving her without
the electricity of his soul.
It had powered all her years with him.
I promised her I would
and moved on in the grocery
to finger ripened mangoes pensively.

Several weeks went by before
I could make myself approach
her door, knocking with a sense
of dread. She seemed surprised
that I had come and took me
laughing, to her laundry room
where neatly tied in bundled

onion sacks, the bulbs were dried
and labeled, one by one.
"It's how he would have done."
She sighed and offered me some daffodils.
"I'm tired of digging holes."
We chatted briefly and I went on
to plant the bulbs around our home.
I set the Canna lilies with care
outside the bathroom window
where I'd see them blooming
several times a day.

Imagine my surprise come June
when glancing out the window
purple gladiolas stood erect beneath the sun
like young soldiers gathered there
to salute a fallen one.

In a Morning's Gardening

When sleepy mockingbirds
begin their pre-dawn twittering
robins, black-capped yellow chickadees
and song sparrows know they must sing
up the sun. I lie wandering between
the place of dreams where not knowing
is the entrance fee, and his strong hand
gentled in sleep over mine.
The day will be hot. The flats
of marigolds, rose coneflowers, lavender,
lipstick and white impatiens, wait.

I slip on shorts and Tee
and ease into the dusky garden beds
to deadhead pansies brightening.
Snipping off the leggy stems
I plunge them wide-eyed into water
'til the old blue beach pail glows
purple, white and yellow mingling.

I set them in the shade beneath the river birch
and take impatiens to their garden bed
noticing the patterned burrowings raised
like veins on the back of my hands...
my mother's hands when I thought she was old.

What creatures, mole, chipmunk or vole
creep within these subterranean arteries
domed and threading plant to plant?
Some I'd set into the earth only a week ago
— the healthy strawflowers drooping now
the clump of tiger lilies I'd moved in early spring
still contemplating when to bloom
today, one limp and yellowing
a rounded tunnel leading to its stem.
I stamp it down, the soft earth
flattening beneath my shoe.
While working up a hole with cow manure
and lime, from the corner of my eye
the earth is rising once again. Scorning
this pastoral scene I stab
and stab until the earth is still

until this paroxysm of the Furies spent
returns to dormancy and I, to brood
to weigh a new-fledged certainty;
I loved my children with a fierceness
such as this when they were

vulnerable as these plants
and realize with something of a chill
I could have killed for them.

Confused, unsettled by the casual
destruction of these helpless living things
by creatures ordained to thrive on them,
and my deranged entanglement in death;
by beauty seen and unseen colliding
at this intersection of love and sudden violence,
I pull the hose to water purple salvia
Texas blue bonnets, pink whirling butterflies —
and learn from them as from the moon
we daily die and dying, live to bloom.
I make a bed of marigolds to sleep
and waken mirroring the sun.

So much life lived
in a morning's gardening.

Owed to the Sweet Potato

this apology for centuries
of benign neglect by bards
and minstrels caroling its praise.
We picked one fat and long
from the bin to go with that
pork tenderloin waiting for the grill.
I rubbed this tubered comma
well with oil, placing under it
a piece of foil knowing it soon
would ooze, as it softened
like a mother's heart.
We opened up this safe-
deposit of the sun and
after buttering and tasting it
agreed it had become
an exclamation mark!

Carolina Wren

When the old white wicker planter
lost its legs to rot this spring
I set it on the back porch bench
to pot it up with pink Diascia,
velvet burgundy petunias
and sweet potato vine.

Under my kitchen window
in this summer of two thousand and three
while the CIA is dreaming of a way
of staking bets on terrorist attacks
a Carolina wren, forsaking shrub and tree
has built her nest deep in the heart
of my throbbing petunia plants.

Though she roofed it patiently with moss
a bright and whiskered green
she sits within her bonny home
a nervous queen, and scolds

when I approach to trim
the wracks of ruined bloom.

I am amazed by her fidelity.
Through thunder blasts
explosive cracks of lightning
and stinging rain —
through baking sun and every
banging pot and pan
she manages to prevail.
I tune to public radio and
play her Grieg and Mendelsohnn.

Yesterday, a minute twittering began
as did her industry in entomology.
Shedding motherhood, this bustling artisan
and her brood will soon be gone.
I shall miss her when her job is done.

Geography of Trees

Maple, cherry, apple, oak and pine
hickory, walnut, elm, ash and birch
put me in mind of faithful families
dressing up and getting off to church
on time even though they're
tempted to sleep in. Their names
march down the tongue
like children lining up at school
row by row, practicing the disciplines
of stop and go, hush and single file
and mind, wait quietly until
you are dismissed. These proper
hardwoods roofed, tabled, floored,
cookied and apple pied, make the New
Englander, Mid-Westerner at home.

Seeds blown across the tossing
salt spray waves from tropic
Caribbean islands to our southern shores

grow into trees whose aptitude
is breaking all the rules;
bursting into bud or leaf year 'round
arms raised, trunks swaying a mean merengue
they fling their rhumba skirts
of rumpled blossoms, brazenly flirting
with the blue astonished sky.

Such abandonment cares not a whit
about respect. Listen to them carry on —
creaking, moaning, beating out
the rhythm of their names — the gilded
satin leaf... tabebuia... jacaranda... bouganvilla
the towering mahoghany... royal ponciana
royal palm... sapodilla... frangi pangi
lignum vitae... and the gumbo limbo tree
cha-cha-cha!

This Great White Pine

Thunder cracking its wicked whip
rumbled up the valley of night.
Rain rode a wild stallion bareback
galloping along the cliffs of sleep.
After breakfast, our neighbor came by
as though he owed us an explanation.
She's got to go. She's leaning more
each day. They'll be here in the morning.
He sighed and turned away.

Not knowing how to say goodbye
to such a monolith as this
great white pine, one of a pair
whose span of life has paralleled
the thrills and insults of my own and more,
I left the house for some mundane
chore I can't recall, imagining
the breathless vacuum of an elder
sister's mortal fall, her life un-spun
leaving me alone.

When I returned, the whining
of the chipper shutting down
bruised the air, a fury of final
raking was underway and when
the men had gone, I went
to see where this great tree
of eighty feet or more had been.

I found the sky wiped clean
but found as well, spread down
the gently sloping hill, its negative
imprinted whole — grass growing
all around the etching of each branch
no longer soughing in the wind.

In Memoriam

for Helena Owen; 1911-2001
for Karin Cox; 1942-2001

Wondrous falls strung
along this river's wild meanderings
framed by hardwoods
towering pine, new leafing rhododendron
trembling against the sky,
to these thundering falls, I sing.
I sing to all the silent droplets
chained and greenly curtaining

to all eddies and rivulets preceding
gathered unto these furious falls
white crowning ancient granite shelves
moss blanketed and lushly ferned
where stubborn laurel
root and bloom and thrive.

They fall — no thought of release
no letting go — and fall
tumbling on to boil

in steaming cauldrons
carved by the eternal
constancy of things
until whirling
churning
they join again
that endless energy
the rhythmic ebb and flow
silent, deep and strong
that quietly collects itself
moves steadily along.

Mother

*from the old song "Annie Laurie"

Maxwelton's braes are bonny
where early falls the dew...*
Her kitchen sink songs fluttered
over us like a blessing veil
her laughter was a comforter
we wrapped ourselves in,
took to our beds at night.
But this Dorothy from Kansas
who married the wizard of Oz
left her sparkling red shoes
her yellow brick road
her laughter, at the door
of death's long hall named Wait
where Annie Laurie broke
all her promises.

Thirteen years she roamed
from wall to wall
searching for that other door.
"Where am I?" The question
hung before her like a miner's lamp
searching for ore. "Where am I?
I want to go home."

She could still recall she'd learned
to read on Longfellow's primer; told
how she'd draw us close beside the fire —
the gnarled limbs gathered
by old Nokomis along the shores
of Gitche Gumee — so we could feel
with Hiawatha the wonder
of the moon and stars
the wide-eyed owl
watching, cooing in the night.

There was no other door, no exit sign.
Dorothy roosted quietly
in a far-off tree until
the feather of her last breath
fluttered into the salty air
and set her free. I wasn't there.

A crackling campfire still kindles
something smoldering in me…
sometimes Annie Laurie
rises on a smoky memory… O,
I wasn't there when she needed me.
I wasn't there.

Invisibilities

Invisible life that sustains all, I awaken to life everything in
every waft of air. The air is life, greening and blossoming;
the waters flow with life: the sun is lit with life. The moon,
when waning, is again rekindled by the sun, waxing with
life once more. The stars shine, radiating with life-light.
                                                    –Hildegard of Bingen

Chameleon, bright green dart
you fly through the emerald air
of swaying sapodilla tree
settle horizontally upon
the gray-barked limb
puddled with splashing sun;
become, in fifteen seconds flat
a peel of bark, invisible.

When Glenis* flings her sharpened dart
soul words come flaming from her lips
come slinky syrup words
flowing down and round her hips
come hungering words searching
for that day we overcome
prideful power words that elevate
her sheroes on the big marquee, and
wake-up-in-the-morning ordinary woman
cooking-eggs-and-grits, getting-kids
to-school woman is gone. Invisible.

Struck by such darts as these
I wonder, are they separate from me?
What lies beyond their horizon line?
And mine? What mysteries of
chemistry churn within unseen?
What of the essence of the air
updrafts and moistures between these darts
and me? Is there not a veiled invisibility
connecting elements I cannot see
raining down and filtering below
slow-percolating up this particular
sapodilla tree, casting unseen ring on ring
like yarn on needle, annually?

What invisibilities inspire
that long legged wordsmith
drunk on metaphor
pounding words like farrier's nails
phrases that leap into the air
from the anvil of her smithery
shooting sparks of images into rooms
and auditoriums igniting effervescent
invisibilities within each listening ear?

And what of the unseen embryo
within a sleeping seed whose waking
finger of green curls into the air
spinning sunlight into stem and vivid petaling
becoming fuchsia cosmos, black eyed susan
holly or distant apple tree?
What attracts the preying mantis
hummingbird, and honey bee
maps their daily journeying...
opens the jasmine bloom

to spoon its fragrance into the eager mouth
of steamy nights beneath the stars…

or opens me to recognize
that wide, deep River through
all creation roaring, scarlet threaded
through the heart of every burning avatar
quiescent pooling, trickling, through me?
What unheard song rises from the sea
to new-hatched turtles blindly scrambling…
or makes the phone's insistent ring
to bring the voice of one appearing
in my heart a blink before?

Something there is, invisible
vectoring between;
riding sun blown or moon-ribboned
highways of the air I breathe and share
with every creature, blossom, tree's
inhaling and exhaling of the air.

The veil is thin. Gauze winding and unwinding
on an endless spool of reciprocity.
So much music! Blues and jazz
and razz-ma-tazz! So much dancing
all around, within me
and between
unseen.

*Glenis Redmond is a teaching,
performing North Carolina poet.*

THREE
AN INCREDIBLE
ART FORM

Tommy and the Generals

*4/9/04, one year to the day
following the fall of Baghdad*

While the full moon rises
over the crest of my hill
I lie and wonder if it got its fill
flying the skies over our desert patrols
over our network centered, high tech
military operations; operations; co-
operations; covert operations
who's doin' the operatin' in this
first high tech war of the information age?
Information age? Here's some information
straight from the horses' mouth;
they're doin' the will, the will
the President's, the Generals' military will
doin' the BIG BOOM SHOCK AND AWE.
"We killed 'em hard
we killed 'em fast
this war's an [incredible] art form!"*
That's what the General on Nova say,
This war's an incredible art form.

Hey diddle diddle, the cat and the fiddle
I got the Cheney, Rumsfeld, Condoleeza, Bush
pre-emptive blues an' I can hear Tommy singin'

"See me, feel me, touch me, heal me."**
See me, feel me, touch me, heal me.

The moon glides trailing her pearly veils
the cow jumps over the moon
the little dog laughs
at the General's boast;
"We split the world into three dimensional boxes
and set our GPS over the sweet spots
into which bombs can be directed."
Boxes, boxes, Jack-in-the-box boxes
three dimensional boxes… the whole wide world
into three dimensional boxes.
And the GPS finds the soft sweet spot
and Little Jack Horner sits in his corner
eating his Christmas pie.

The guns are trained and the bombs
are trained by the GPS for the
BIG BOOM SHOCK AND AWE
and he sticks his thumb in that soft 'sweet spot'
he pulls out a bomb and says, what a good boy am I!
Am I? Am I? What if Mom's in that box
or you or I? And the General say
"Though we failed to achieve Iraqi capitulation
with our BIG BOOM SHOCK AND AWE
our digital tracking of equipment and events
on the battlefield provides
syncronization of asymetric warfare!"

Warfare, warfare, asymetric warfare
warfare, warfare, asymetric wa…
We killed 'em hard
we killed 'em fast

this war's an incredible art form.
That's what the General on Nova say,
"This war's part science, part battery pack
but [damn!] we just keep runnin' out of batteries!"
Jack be nimble, Jack, be quick
Jack, run out to that tank with a candlestick!
An' hey! remind me to buy some more battery stock.
Ah, this war's an incredible art form.
"almost like in the movies or sompin'."

Hey diddle diddle, the cat and the fiddle
I got the Cheney, Rumsfeld, Condoleeza, Bush
pre-emptive blues an' I can hear Tommy cryin'
See me, feel me, touch me, heal me.
See me, feel me, touch me, heal me.

While the full moon's swallowed
by the tall white pine
and the dish runs away with the spoon
the Commander of a Naval ship reveals
Our troops are trained and our sights are trained
and our missiles are trained by the GPS
for the BIG BOOM SHOCK AND AWE...
and we let 'em rip and run for the stairs
to the TV room and lounge
and tune right in to CNN
for THE BIG BOOM SHOCK AND AWE...
one hundred fifty miles away!
THE BIG BOOM SHOCK AND AWE.

And the General say,
(as long as the Energizer bunny don't run down)
"We will see first, we will act first
we will know first, and we will finish decisively."

Decisively! That's what the General on Nova say,
We killed 'em hard, we killed 'em fast
this war's an incredible art form.

Hey diddle diddle, the cat and the fiddle
the cow jumps over the moon
the little dog laughs to see such sport...
and the dish runs away with the spoon.
I got the Cheney, Rumsfeld, Condoleeza, Bush
pre-emptive blues an' I can hear Tommy wailin'
See me, feel me, touch me, heal me.
See me, feel me, touch me, heal me...
heal me... heal me...

Quotes from NOVA, "Battle Plan Under Fire" viewed Feb.2004. Though the General may not have used the word 'incredible' in this context, his demeanor and use of it otherwise makes it an appropriate insertion.

**from the musical "Tommy" by Peter Townshend

Staramajka
Bosnian Grandmother

Remembering the day she hacked
her cherished dresser up for fuel
she digs into the pile of clothes
neat folded in the corner of the room
she used to share with him
until he stole away into the troubled air.
She had lay on him to keep him warm
his foul breath rasping on her throat
until she whispered in his ear
that he could go.

Memories fly like moths
from deep within the woolen socks
the underwear once sweetly scented
in her Baba's ornate chest
tooled by her father's patient hand
when she was newly born and named.
It, too, is gone to flame.

She draws the golden frame
from deep within the fabric of her life
and tracing it with moaning fingers
bruised by cold, etches the laughing face
upon her heart — her mother, as a child
— tucks the locket trembling
between her withered breasts.

Rumors swirling from the market place…
could it be true?
Her steps are slow, but eager.
Hope is for sale on the street
in mounds of cabbages, potatoes
turnips, even greens, they said.
She rounds the corner, stumbling
and feasts upon the scene —
what it would mean to them
the remnant of her family!

She steps into the noisy throng
oblivious to the shadows circling overhead
and with a hungry eye her quest begins;
a mean selection — parsnips
two limp carrots, onions
that would make a stew alive
yet these humble roots
are not enough to satisfy.

The hope she wants to buy
must glow beyond the day
must be the sun until
this clash of manly will is done.

And then she spies
three tangerines incandescent
as that luminary in the sky.
Swallowing hard against the flood
that rises 'round her lips and tongue
and clutching at the treasure
near her heart, she reaches out for one
joy rising in her veins like spring
just one for them
   to touch
      to smell
         to ta...

In memory of those who died in the bombing of the
Sarajevo marketplace February 5, 1994

Hide and Seek

*The following three poems visited me in the persona of
a wise woman of the South. Bold with truths that seem
apparent to her, she's quick to observe discrepancies between
who I appear to be and who I am when no one's looking.
She suffers no silencing by disdain or bashful modesty,
saying who she is and what she thinks with good humor
and honesty. I welcome her back any time for more girl talk.*

Hey, Mr. Smug! I see you hidin' behind that Bush!
What you hidin' from, Mr. Smug?
Always playin' the same ol' tunes across your jug
ya' got ever'one out there trained like ducks —
buy it, use it, bust it up
throw it in the garbage truck

said, buy it use it, bust it up
throw it in the garbage truck!
Hey Smug, don't see them diggin'
no land fill in your back yard.

Oh yeah, Wall Street's in the black
and you so satisfied.
Drivin' that BMW make you real dignified
thinkin' Easy Jesus pin his badge a' truth on you.
Your black an' white game drivin' us insane!
Got no time to socialize
hear somebody's cries
look into their eyes, sympathize.
You like your feelin's neat, like gin

an' under control. Never dare to let us in
show your soul. What you hidin' from, Mr. Smug?
What you hidin' from? One, two, three on Smug!

Well, what you hidin' from Roly Poly?
Gotta' get your fix down at the mall
shoppin' shoppin' shoppin' 'til your arches fall!
Arms laced across your tummy chuggin' out in front
hips too many double dips
sparkle come into ya' eye settin' down to pizza pie
polished off an' cravin' more.
Honey, some kinda' deep down hunger
knockin' at your door? I see ya'
pour yourself another shot a' gin
light up that fag an' suck it in
blowin' smoke thick as sin.
Now ever'one love a jolly clown
but honey, wantin' wantin' wantin'
gonna' put you six foot down!

Roly Poly, I know you ain't dumb
Roly Poly, what you hidin' from?
One, two three on Roly!

Now what you hidin' from Proud Betty
head up in the clouds?
Thinkin' you a notch above the crowds
thinkin' you the judge 'a ever'one's prose
lookin' down that long, white ski slope 'a your nose.
Reachin' up to touch the hem 'a God
don' even see them flames shootin' outa your toes!

Honey, you so vain, won't even use
them hearing aids or cane.
Standin' in the need a' your disguise
Sugar, what you doin' best is criticize
opinionize. Hey, Ms. Polish Up Your Intellect
strut your stuff, be correct
thinkin' that book before your face
bring you respect. Thinkin' you so good
no time to waste out in the neighborhood.
Readin' readin' readin' all the time
tryin' ta' figure out what lie between the line.
Don'cha know it time to rise an' shine?
Rise an' shine sublime, divine!
Wake up, Proud Betty Know it All
or you be headin' for a fall.
What you hidin' from, Proud Betty?
What you hidin' from? One, two, three on Betty!

Well, well, well, what you hidin' from, Sad One?
Always lookin' back at what has been and gone
or worryin' 'bout the what to come.
Ain't nothin' beatin' on your drum.
Sorrow seem to be the price 'a life for you
seein' sadness ever'where
always wearin' that empty stare
sleepin' off the day's despair
kicked back in your loungin' chair.
What you hidin' from, Sad One?
What you hidin' from?
One, two, three on Sad One!

Hey! What you hidin' from Scaredy Cat?
'Fraid 'a steppin' on the sidewalk crack
cuz for sure you gonna break your mama's back.

Ohhh! Don' take a breath while goin'
by the graveyard or you gonna die!
'Fraid that bully's gonna beat you up
'fraid you got no friends to fill your cup
'fraid someone's gonna snatch your chile
criticize; make fun 'a you a while
steal your goods; knock you in the eyes
strap on some bombs and terrorize!
'Fraid 'a livin', 'fraid 'a dyin'
'fraid 'a givin', 'fraid 'a tryin'
what you hidin' from, Scaredy Cat?
One, two, three on Scaredy!

Well, what you hidin' from, Frustration's Chile?
Anger sparkin' from your lips
fury ballin' up your fingertips
rage snappin' like the sheets out on the line!
Ever'one aroun' you feel like pickle brine.
Ya' got ta' have your say, get your way
yellin' 'til your lungs go dry
leave you feelin' sad and wonderin' why
no one love you anymore.
Feel like walkin' out the door.
What you hidin' from, Frustration's Chile?
Huh? What you hidin' from?
One, two, three I see you! I see you! I see you!

Hey ever'one! Come on in! Alle, alle in free!
Don'cha hear that dinner bell?
Time ta' quit the game, run on home
run like from hell! I know ya' hot as sin
but Mama callin' all us in.

G'on now, wash up your hands an' face
listen to your Daddy sayin' grace.
Help y'self to table set for you.

I said, help y'self to table set for you!
Comfort food in ever' bowl
greens... Oh Lordy, greens
stirred up with wine, vinegar an' oil.
Honey, Mama's bread can raise the dead
eat up 'til you feelin' full.
Oh yeah, then help clear the table
wash up pots an' pans, put on the tea
then set y'selves down with Mama
an' memorize her recipe.

What's that, hon? Oh, you know the one
'bout that wide, deep river runnin' through you
s'posed to hang out there 'til the grass turns blue.
Now honey, if you lookin' for that river
'stead 'a the bog yo' in
listen up to Mama callin' all us in!
G'on now, run on home. G'on home.
Home's the place we oughta' be.
Alle, alle in free
   Alle, alle in free
      Alle, alle in free…..free….free…
               free… free...
C'mon home. Mama callin' *you.*

Girl Talk

Hey Sistah!
Y'all got time for some girl talk?
Cuz honey, I been needin' me some
down home, back porch, set down girl talk.
Now you guys can listen, too
but I really wanna' talk jus' girl talk.
Honey, you know what it feel like
when you been raised by God-man-he?
Girl, stand tall and hold your shoulders straight!
An' don't you be fussin' when he stay out too late.
Better mind your P's and Q's
jus' get used to payin' your dues
cuz that Big Daddy in the Sky
watchin' every wiggle of your thigh.
Girl, you know, it feel like, Girl, you better
get down on your knee, bow your head
close your eyes when you be talkin' to me.

Now, when you been raised on God-man-he
honey, here's what it feel like to me!
Girl, you better do it right — (whatever "it" is)
bow your head to pray
read your Bible every day
an' listen hard to what the preacher say.
Now I can see you guys roll your eyes
I can hear you say, " Git over it!
Why don'cha jus' git over it!
Always been that way, always gonna be that way.
Git over it." I say, 'hain't always been that way, honey

an you jus' hold your britches
while we talkin' girl talk. Three…
four thousand years you had your way
it time for girl talk.

Ya' see, we starved, ain't we Sugar
for the sweet taste a' holy woman names!
Bent like beggars, we tired a' gleanin'
all those testi…ments to God-man-he
(all those books they read in semen…ary).
Our fingertips been rubbed smooth against the page
lookin', lookin', lookin' for the feminine divinity!
We be like bees, hungry for the nectar in her flower.
Thirsty, for the juice a' woman talk, woman power.
An' when we pray, oh honey, the sound a' *She*
Sh…Sh…Sh…eeeeeee! Oooooooeeeeee!
Soun' jus' like heaven to me.

Yeah, Mama-god-she can make us whole.
She leadeth me beside the still waters
She restoreth my soul. Restoreth *my* soul, honey!
She leadeth me along the path a' goodness
for her names' sake. *Her* names' sake!
Somethin' right about the way that feels
the way that sends shivers from
my head right down through my heels.
All scrunched up inside we say
yea, though I walk through the valley
of the shadow of death, like we thinkin'
it jus' for dyin' day. Honey! We walkin'
that valley every day! Every day, birthin'
bloomin', dyin' fronta' our eyes, every day.
Why we so scared?

My Mama-god's arms and heart, they comfort me.
Yeah, Mama-god-she, she comfort you…
oh, she comfort me. Ever' day she set her table
fronta' you. What's that, honey?
Now, you thinkin' white linen
fine china, Pier One silverware?
You thinkin' you an' Mama-god-she
gonna set y'selves down an'
have your own private tea party?
Mmm Mmmm Baby! You got that wrong!
Ever' day she set her table fronta' you
fronta' me; table a' this day
table a' right now, fronta' me.

We say, in the presence a' my enemies
like we thinkin' Iraq! Or that… hmph!.. frien'
whose whisperin' stab me in the back
or some po' chile whose Mama blind on crack.
No, no, honey, she mean cast your eyes
into the mirror! Look real deep and see…
Now honey, I ain't 'bout to tell you what enemy
you gonna see! That between you and Mama-god-she
but when your heart be feelin' all clean and free
you know what Mama-god-she gonna do?
She gonna pour her oil all over you
She even gonna fill your cup 'til it overflow!
Oh, honey, that the way you gonna know
never no doubt about it, ya hear me now?
Never no doubt about it, that her goodness
and mercy, they gonna flow.

Say what? Do I hear you thinkin'
Mama gonna set her goodness and mercy
down fronta' you like some pot-luck cass-a-role?

Like some big pan a' baklavah?
Oh, no, honey! Her goodness an' mercy
they gonna follow *you*!
It's outa' *you* they gonna flow
cuz she made you a home right from the start.
She make you a home right here in her heart.

Oh, I know. Some a' you guys 'n
some a' you nice ladies, too
thinkin' we barkin' up the wrong tree.
Can'cha see? The flavor of her on our tongues
on your tongues, like dark chocolate
melt right down to our toes.
We can hear her sayin'
There, there, chile, I know how it goes.
She melt right into our dried up souls
an' feed us her dark sweet a while
like Mama's milk comfort a squallin' chile.

Mmmm? Oh I 'spect, after a while, hard to say
fifty, hundred years or so hangin' out
in the heart a' Mama-god-she
while she be rockin', rockin' to an' fro
(soun' like pure luxury to me, honey)
yeah, fifty, hundred years or so
we might jus' then begin to know
that she… is he, an' they… is we
an' holy be beyond the beyond
an' within' the within' of everythin'
an' she be wantin' us to come on in to play!
An' after a-rockin' an' a-talkin' an' a-listenin'
a spell, go out with us into the day
to be Mama-god-she, God-man-he
knowin' Mamas don' approve a' messin'

with guns and bombs, cuz someone's chile
always standin' on the hurtin' end
an' she be wantin' all a' us to be a frien'.

So listen up now, to some girl talk
an' like they say, honey, if ya' gonna
talk the talk, ya' gotta walk the walk.
Now if your gonna take this walk with me
try to get your head around it
try to get your heart around it
I said, try to get your head around it
try to get your heart around it
that she is he, an' they is we
an' holy be beyond the beyond
an' within the within of every thin'
everythin'! Ev-'ry-thin'!
an she be wantin' us to come on in ta' play
an' after a-rockin' an' a-talkin' an' a-listenin'
a spell, go out with us into the day
to be Mama-god-she, God-man-he
knowin' — now listen up honey, an' get this straight!
knowin' that Mamas do not approve a' messin'
with guns an' bombs, cuz someone's chile,
*some*one's chile always standin' on the hurtin' end
an' she be wantin' all a' us
    all a' us
        all a' us
She be wantin' all a' us to be a frien'.

Woman, Who Are You?

Honey, I knows who I is!
See this hair white like ivory snow
Mama useta' beat to brush the spotted carpet clean.
Hair done its share a' bed rock, half-crock
peacock struttin' pillow talk! Hair
tired 'a envy eyes, bottle dyes 'n peroxide
tryin' to make it seem like young
an' what it ain't. Hair, white
like the Goose that lay the golden egg
tellin' me an' all the world who I is —
a woman of a certain jus' right size
what you see ain't even half 'a me
a woman of years an' ripe with wise
who's got that hidden fountain
sparklin' in her eyes.

Sugar, see this face lookin' like a road map
windin' through the Amazon
through all those places done and gone
of no return. All those
twistin' windin' grindin' places
all those smilin' cryin' laughin'
lovin' dyin' places we been before we
come on home. Ya see, this face that percolates
resuscitates and activates can be jus' like
a traffic cop. Put up the big red STOP!
or smile the amber slow... grin the green.
Don' let nothin' come between me an' joy, boy
cuz' I'ze a woman of a certain jus' right size

what you see ain't even half 'a me
a woman of years and ripe with wise
who's got that hidden fountain
sparklin' in her eyes.

Honey, see these breasts? Use ta' be firm
with jus' the right move an' jiggle
groove an' wiggle, then spent some time
servin' up all that baby fat, love sucky
milk drippin', sleep druggin', baby lovin' ju-ju
heavy like two dead ripe honey-dew.
Ain't what they used to be, honey, they still
full 'a sympathy; they still soft and warm
know how to perform; a pair 'a perfect miracles
when someone sufferin' one a' life's storms
needin' somethin' like the feast a' reason
an' the flow 'a the soul. Somethin' to rest
a weary head upon. Come lay your ear on
somethin' cushiony and make acquaintance
with that drum beatin' rhythm steady like a
sunny warm thunderstorm. Transform
your blues 'til you regained your gentility
recultivated your amenity, your amiability.
It's me you need to come an' see, honey
'cuz I'ze a woman of a certain jus' right size.
What you see ain't even half 'a me
a woman of years and ripe with wise
who's got that hidden fountain
sparklin' in her eyes.

Take a gander at this belly
round as mother earth
belly been givin' birth, an' givin' birth
an' givin' birth, an' givin' birth!

This belly, first cradle of a mama
nurse, frien' an' volunteer
first home of a brilliant tunnel engineer
first rockin' chair of a heavy duty Dad
an' manufacturer; first swimmin' pool
of a man workin' like a fool ta' get peas
n 'taters 'n broccoli in ever' home and school.

Now, you thinkin' I done with givin' birth?
So tired an' old, ain't got much worth?
Honey, this belly round as mother earth
hold that Goose that lay the golden egg
an' Sugar, that Goose ain't white — mm..mmmm!
no, she ain't white, she full a' light!
She whisper an' croon… she listen an' commune.
She call me by name to quit the game!
She agitates
         she incarnates
                  she incubates
                           she animates!
She knowin' alla' me an' alla' you.
You hearin' me now? She knowin' alla' me
an' alla' you! An' givin' birth is what she do
when she meet a woman of a certain
jus' right size. A woman of years
an' ripe with wise. Oh honey,
she be that hidden fountain
sparklin' in my eyes.

Woman Waking

*Commissioned for a
croning ceremony in Peru*

Woman, waking from
a sleep-walker's restless sleep
rise to the birthing of the crone!
Cast off that long and tattered scarf of red
your rumpled milk-soured bed, with gratitude.
Score-keeping's done.
A bowl you've become, slow filled
poured out and ready to be rung.
Adorn yourself!
Sophia's hooded robe of gray
long awaits the you
you never knew.

Draw deep your breath, and headlong
sail her golden vessel, reliable and strong.
You sail not alone. Raven, bright-eyed
imp and scavenger, with awkward dance
and caw, commissions you — perches light
upon your shoulder teaching death's
dark secrets in the night.
Snake, devouring her tail
transforms the bitter grail brim'd
with perpetual perishing to life anew.
Raise high the luminary of years
well lived, and living into future mysteries

cast wisdom's raveled light along
the shadowed path in front of you.

Shamans we, keepers of the sacred flame
stir the bubbling cauldron
blackened by the refiner's fiery blaze
distilling disciplines we've grown to claim —
patience and the ready ear, the sound
of our own voice no longer censored by our fear
the outreached hand, willingness to persevere
the steady, silent gaze. Rooted deep
and strong, we stand
tree-like and tall
  speak out
    command.

This ancient recipe, flavored by the sweet
and pungent brie of contemplation
awakening quiet powers
ripened deep within, makes us whole
creates the alchemy of potent medicines
for healing earth and heart, mind and soul.

The price for voyaging is dear. Fearless
navigate new mysteries with her
discover secret passages
expansive rivers broad and long.

When the great round turns
to fling you fully croned
through narrowing straits of years
across the wide and riddled ocean of decline
she weaves for you a cushioned bower
of moss to smooth the bed of death
her belly large with light and laughter
pearled moon-beams on her breath.

Woman, waking from a great sleep
rise to the birthing of the crone!
You join a learned company
a vast and veiled hagiology
a sisterhood that circumnavigates with you
through days and dreams unknown.
Draw deep your breath
sing reverently your evensong.
Hoist the weighty grindlestone
and sail Sophia's golden vessel
reliable and strong.

Rhubarb

Emboldened by the banked
and glowing sun
drawn down through rocketing
green, your roots aim deep
for targets unseen
like arrows shot into obscurity.

I am your devotee!
So unassumingly you make
the cycling of each summer's day
your wheel, spinning manure and clay
into belly laughs of green.

I come to you with regularity
to mine the sun, your everyday
simplicity, your ruby shafts
of tart-tongued succulence pied
or sauced with Mother's recipe.
Ours is a credulous dependency.

August Trip

I dive into the warm heart of tomato,
chambered nautilus dreaming marinara
dreams under a jaguar sun
that stalks my humped and dimpled back,
cherries my cheeks. Rain knuckles my face.
My tongue runs with memory of basil breeze
okra, chive. I spiral in, drowning
in seed-slimed, lightning grizzled
thunder drenched alkahest;
snake through the collared nub
where secrets sung between stem
and blossom still resonate; begin the slide
down emerald corridors staked and tied;
rapture my way into root lips
sucking intoxicating juices of meadow
cow, forest trail, sparks of stars soil strewn
and beetle shouldering moon glistened
dung balls along the brown surf of worms
thirsting for late summer rains.

Satisfied, I retrace my way until
a holy stillness steadies me within
vibrations still rippling from

that first awakening of dry seed.
I am expansion… contraction
exaltation of simultaneous opposites
thrusting up to pierce the truth of sun
and down to drink the dark genius of soil.
Here, at the heart of seed
Infinite Silence yearns, radiant
with yellow blossom eyes
and breathing green fire!

Connemara After Dark*

One night, long after sleep
had tied its final knot
my pen slipped out the door
hiked down the valley
through the meadow
at the bottom of the hill
crossed Mud Creek bridge
on Middleton and hurried
up the gravel road.

Calves, constellations
of darker black against
their mothers' flank
lowed quietly. A few fireflies
still blinked from deep within the grass.

The moon cut a trail to
Little River road where
Glassy Mountain shone
like the sleepless eye of God.

My truant pen began to glide
up hill and down, encouraged
by the quiet rustling of rhododendron,
a dog's short bark from within
a sleeping house.

It came upon a twinkling through
the trees; stars fallen, floating
on the lake that baptized
our great poet's later years.

Excited now, it circumscribed
the lake — pausing here and there
picking up vibrations of
that other's pen still quivering
in the peaceful air

climbed the rocky rooted trail
paused again, entered slow
upon wide thighs of rock still warm
deep sinew'd, lichen laced;
the blue-green bloom thriving
on the birthing heat of all that
line and verse and form.

Spurred on by a peculiar urgency
my pen emerged from trees
deep rooted as the poet's home
glowing there on the mountain side
like a mother's wide apron
joyful thrown around the visitor
or covering the crisp, clean dress
of solitude.

The moon, now hiking up
Big Glassy trail, stretched
out a finger for my pen to ride
into the master's third floor
writing room; set down

a pool of light upon
the well worn desk beside

his half smoked cigar
his Remington, his black pencils
sharpened as he left them there.
"The peoples' poet"
the power of him still resonating
in the room transfixed
my quaking pen
filled it with profound humility.

How it returned that night
to me I've never learned.
It left the lines "Mud Creek
still talking in its sleep;
wooden mailboxes steaming
in the slanted rays of sun."

I found it sleeping sound
beside my chair
this poem near complete
upon the table there.

*Now a National Historic Site, Connemara was home to
Carl Sandburg and his family in Flat Rock, NC*

From the poem…

Love Humming in a Nearby Room

It's a long ago memory…
rhythm of the rocking chair
the future wrapped in hope
warm against my heart.
My days, like doors opened
to the brightness of each dawn
were bolted safe at night to shelter me
from any passing storm.
The world, a thoroughfare connecting
bedroom, kitchen sink, the lullabies,
the rocking chair, the grocery store
and cries of war but whispers in the air.

Though now my days, like doors
still open to the dawn, there is no bolt
to keep me safe from storm.
The world turns, I wake
to find the human race burning;
hate spun like cotton candy

handed to the young.
America, our little piggy
goes to market like a sidewalk whore.
Doctor says so much bacteria
don't go in the ocean
with an open sore.
Tropic forests are ablaze
the Arabs want to buy our shore.
Icebergs are melting and we're
fighting over water now.
Malaria and HIV is killing half of Africa
and bird flu looms. I hear
woeful sighs from every living
breathing and inert domain.

What can I do but rise at dawn
to murmur prayers, gather round
a table pot luck style, rock a baby
touch an arm, look into a troubled eye
share a smile, a story over candlelight
read a poem, gently bid good night?
These are the lullabies still rising sweet
that when I sing, I — slayer and slain
fallen, rising, slow advancing
down the twisted lane — become again
love humming in a nearby room.

O You Braided Waters

of rivers, poets and histories

O you braided waters
trickling cold and clear
as the morning air stubbed
with smoke and common conversation
I praise you, the long path taken
issuing from the tribal throat and drum
the fractured rock of royalty
the stubborn will of vulgar peasantry.

I praise you wicked waters belching
putrid ships of frightened women;
one clinging to five children
and the family silverware.
Thrown onto this foreign shore
with nothing more than hope
shoe-leather will, gritty intellect
and courage to endure amidst
the grizzled caravan of strangers
heading west, they followed you;
your golden promises
your shining tongue, uncoiling
beneath the frizzled sun.

You carried them bucket
by leaden bucket across
the tortured magnificence
of this fretted generous land,
brought me to a curious shore to
join a different caravan.
I praise you deep well waters I
pumped by hand at the kitchen sink
into the honest cup of child-hood days
cart-wheeling now down
forested mountainsides into the pools
and tides of every day spilling
through the narrow channel of my pen.

I ride this unruly ship tossing me
toward waters still uncharted
dip my oar into the ink
of your dark swells and swamps.
I praise your height and depth
your ways of walking small

across the land; your lyric gush and flow
your wild, restless meanderings
covered, bridged and dammed.
(They climb on you, shout "oooo"
and "ahhhhh," move quickly on.)
I praise your search for nooks
and crevices, your hospitality
to creatures near extinct;
salamanders, gray wolf, owl and whale;
the reverence you inhere
in droplet fallen through a gaze
fast disappearing in my own

as in the broken open softening
of each hard kernel grown to bloom.

We carry you disguised in piss and plastic
you flamboyant peacock, squawking
down long halls of respectability
poking into torpid rooms
tail fanned with images
and reflections moistening
the soul. I praise all your paralysis
and power, your voice of hope
singing through the brilliance
of every fall, chanting winter's
sleeping song, humming seed into joy.

O you braided waters
trickling cold and clean
you carriers of the dream
you tributaries and rivulets spread
far across the land; flow on.
I praise your deep interior stir
your splash, your roar,
the beauty you ignite in your
gentle-misted fall through light.

Notes

ONE

The Church of Poetry began after I read the poems and introduction to *Good Poems for Hard Times;* selected by Garrison Keillor (Penguin Group, 2006)

Thoughts Unthought: In lira form, this came after reading Paul Mariani's "The Intensest Rendezvous," on the poems of St. John of the Cross. *Parabola:* Vol. 30 #2, 2005; which included St. John's "Noche oscura".

On Truth of Skies and Trees: inspired by George MacDonald's essay; "The Imagination"

Old Speech: followed a trip to Kenya and Ken Hawkinson's article "Old Speech" in *Parabola;* June 1994. Griots are the story-tellers, the carriers of tradition.

Karen Armstrong: with thanks to Karen Armstrong for her notable book, *A History of God.*

TWO

Hitch-hike the Hubble: For ten days in Dec. 1995, the NASA Hubble Space Telescope, orbiting far above the earth's atmosphere, pointed its lens toward what seemed an "uncluttered" portion of sky in the constellation Ursa Major. Astronomers narrowed the focus of the telescope to a tiny speck of black sky about the size of a dime at 75 feet.

From Jacob Needleman's *A Sense of the Cosmos: Scientific Knowledge and Spiritual Truth;* (Monkfish Publishing)

Light: owes its existence to Christian Wertenbaker's "The Eye of the Beholder;" *Parabola*; Vol. 26 No.2. He writes: "Where-ever molecules are vibrating, which is everywhere, light is being produced. [It is the] universal medium of attraction and repulsion, transformation and exchange."

This Elegant Adagio: I was remembering, as I did my laps, a statement I'd seen somewhere to the effect that of all the species of life on earth, it can be said only of humans that if we were to disappear from the face of the earth, all other forms of life would benefit.

Antarctica: written on a napkin after viewing the film by the same name at an Imax theater in Feb. 1992.

THREE

Tommy and the Generals: The NOVA quotes came from the show "Battle Plan Under Fire" I watched in Feb. 2004.

Acknowledgements

I am particularly indebted to my friend Therese B. Dykeman; poet, philosopher, editor of books on women philosophers, experienced adjunct professor and friend, whose critique helped immensely in bringing this book to publication.

My thanks to many encouragers; to the faithful who come to hear my poems into life; to the brave who invite me into their lives not knowing what they are about to get; and especially to those who want the poems in hand as food for the journey.

About the Author

In addition to her print and audio materials, Martha O. Adams offers poetry in performance; programs for groups, classes, or retreats. She is available to bring her play <u>She Rises Through the Sickle Moon</u>, to groups wishing to participate in using this dramatic device to learn about the stories of women who shaped the history of nations around the world.

Adams lives with her husband in Flat Rock, NC and can be reached by contacting House of Myrrth; Myrrth@bellsouth.net

Praise for
What Your Heart Needs to Know

"THIS POETRY IS GENEROUS; gives us wings, fins, and honey for the journey. Adams' images resonate with echoes of forgotten wisdom. Her gritty poems hold war before us in the terrible immediacy of the intimate. To read her poetry is to be changed."

–Alice Abel Kemp, Ph.D., Emeritus Professor of Sociology and Women's Studies, University of New Orleans

"ADAMS' POEMS ARE FEARLESS, YET RENDERED WITH HUMILITY. They pose questions, present challenges, and urge us to blossom, to sing. She shines her poetic light on hypocrisy, inviting participation, recognition and change. Filled with jazz/hip-hop musicality, her poems seek to keep the human in humanity, the moral in morality, and family in all the faces of humankind."

–Richard Fewell; Playwright; Who's Who Among African Americans

"ADAMS WEAVES HER WORDS WITH DELICATE CARE, giving readers a great depth of character and strong sense of place in each poem, taking us to oases of beauty and serenity, and also into the darkest corners of the human experience."

–Mary Garrison; Times-News columnist and author

ADAMS' POEMS SPEAK TO THE HEART; make me want to take action.
A consummate writer and poet, her words beg great applause."

–Barbara Lange; artist, writer, teacher

"I'M GLAD THIS IS WHAT ADAMS HAS DECIDED SHE'S SUPPOSED
TO BE DOING; giving us pause to pay attention to ourselves, our
world."

–Corrie Norman, Ph.D., Education Director, diningforwomen.org

"ADAMS' POWERFUL VOICE ELEGANTLY AND ARTFULLY
JUXTAPOSITIONS a serene love for the natural world against the
injustices of the world and the follies of humankind. The depth of her
emotion is rich and riveting."

–Kathleen Barnes; author and editor of books on
natural health and sustainable living.

"ADAMS PACKS A POWERFUL PUNCH; deftly takes you to many
places: to the natural world, into your social conscience, to look in a
mirror, and above all, to the heart."

–William T. Garrison, DDS; lifelong avid reader

Also by Martha O. Adams

Poetry:
PEELING THE RIND
Hailed as food for reflection faithful to the vision of
feminist ethics, these poems link together women of spirit
past and present. Published by House of Myrrth;
1st edition 2000; 2nd edition 2003

SHE RISES THROUGH THE SICKLE MOON
Readers' theatre play giving voice to the unsung names and
stories, thoughts and passions of women whose energies
and intellect changed the world; nine Playbooks, boxed;
House of Myrrth; 2003

GIRL TALK,
a CD of poems; performed by the author;
House of Myrrth; 2005

Other:
ALZHEIMER'S DISEASE;
COURAGE FOR THOSE WHO CARE
for caregivers of the Alzheimer's afflicted, 1986, 1st edition
Abbey Press, publisher; 2nd revised edition United Church
Press, publisher; 1999; Available, House of Myrrth.

For information, contact House of Myrrth;
Myrrth@bellsouth.net

CPSIA information can be obtained
at www.ICGtesting.com
Printed in the USA
FFOW02n1857040615
13925FF